UNCOVER HISTORY

THE STONE, BRONZE, AND IRON AGES

CLARE HIBBERT

PowerKiDS press

Published in 2026
by The Rosen Publishing Group, Inc.
2544 Clinton Street, Buffalo, NY 14224

First published in Great Britain in 2023 by Hodder & Stoughton

Series Editor: Lisa Edwards
Series Design and illustration: Collaborate

The text in this book first appeared
in History Detective Investigates: Stone, Bronze and
Iron Age by Clare Hibbert (Wayland).

Cataloging-in-Publication Data
Names: Hibbert, Clare.
Title: The Stone, Bronze, and Iron Ages / Clare Hibbert.
Description: Buffalo, NY : PowerKids Press, 2026. | Series: Uncover history | Includes glossary and index.
Identifiers: ISBN 9781499454604 (pbk.) | ISBN 9781499454611 (library bound) | ISBN 9781499454628 (ebook)
Subjects: LCSH: Civilization, Ancient--Juvenile literature. | Stone age--Juvenile literature. | Bronze age--Juvenile literature. | Iron age--Juvenile literature. | Technological innovations--Juvenile literature.
Classification: LCC CB311.H533 2026 | DDC 930--dc23

Manufactured in the United States of America
CPSIA Compliance Information: Batch #CSPK26. For further information contact Rosen Publishing at 1-800-237-9932.

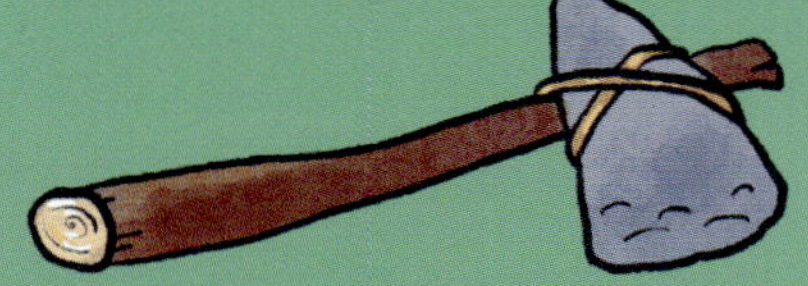

CONTENTS

WHO WERE THE FIRST BRITONS?

Early humans reached Britain at least 800,000 years ago. They may have belonged to a species called *Homo erectus*, which had spread across Europe and Asia from Africa.

Today, there is only one kind of human on earth: *Homo sapiens*. But before we came along, there were many different human species. *Homo erectus* evolved in Africa 1.8 million years ago and was able to make simple stone tools. The period *Homo erectus* lived in is known as the Old Stone Age.

Hunter-gatherers crossed the wide land bridge that still connected Britain to Europe. They followed herds of animals, from deer to mammoths and woolly rhinos, and killed them for their meat and skins.

At night, people made rough shelters or slept in caves. They had fire, but probably couldn't start one. Instead, they found smoldering branches after lightning strikes or wildfires and kept them burning.

The Neanderthals reached Britain 60,000 years ago. They could make fire, and could survive even during ice ages. They buried their dead too.

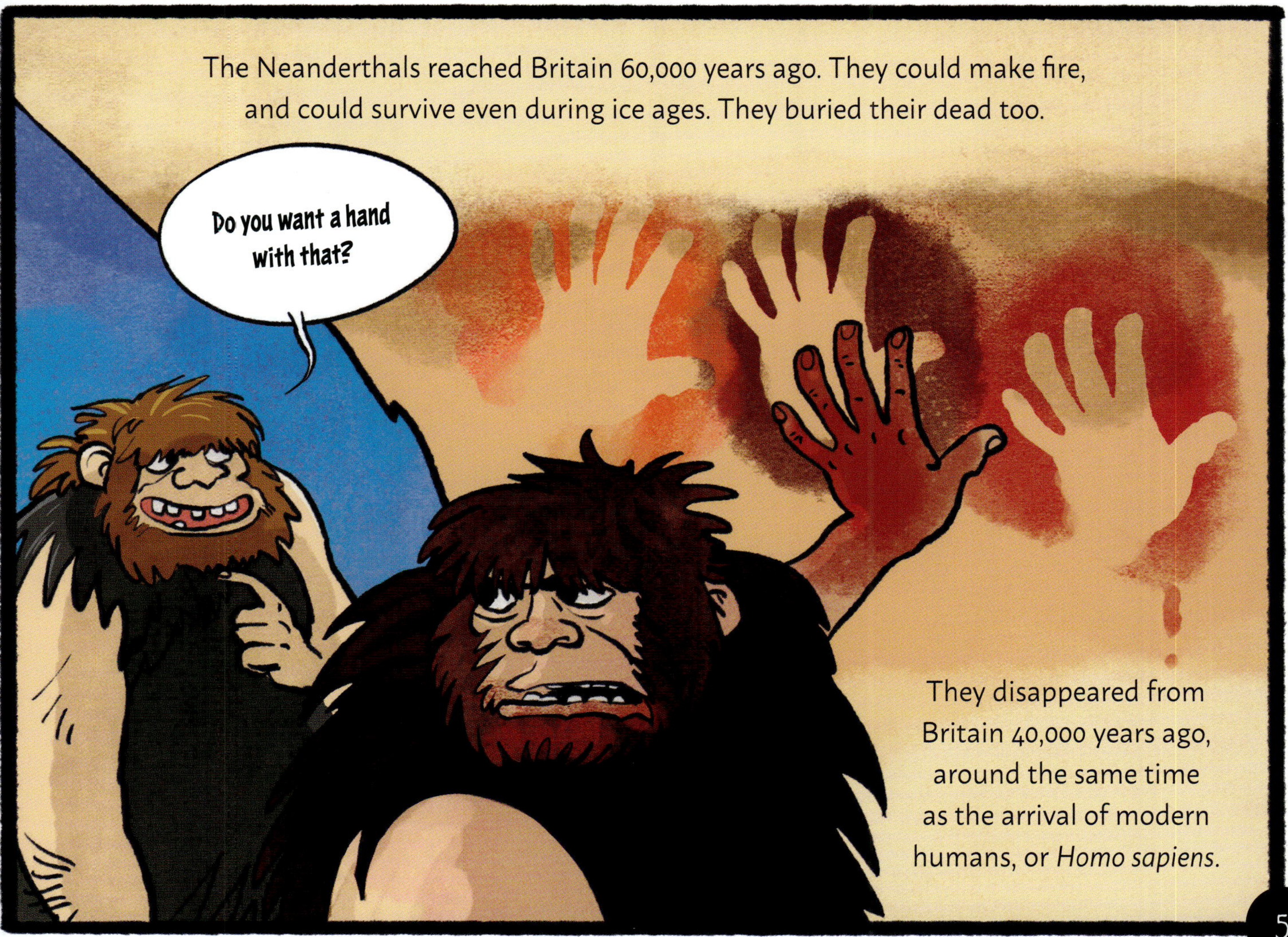

Do you want a hand with that?

They disappeared from Britain 40,000 years ago, around the same time as the arrival of modern humans, or *Homo sapiens*.

When Was the Middle Stone Age?

The period from about 11,500 to 6,000 years ago is known as the Middle Stone Age. People led more settled lives. They cleared woodlands and built sturdier shelters, where they would stay for a few months at a time.

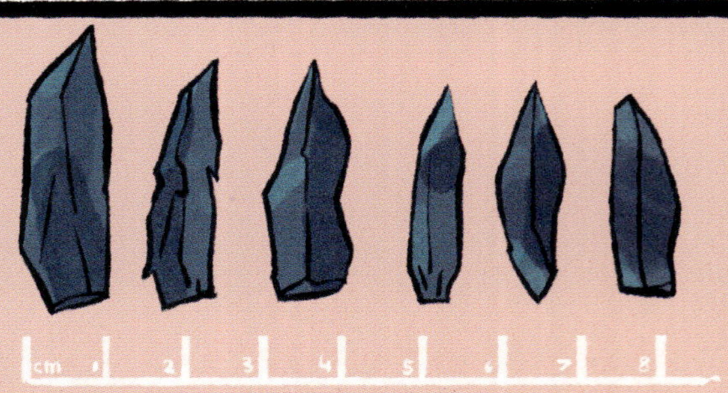

They crafted tiny, sharp flint blades called microliths. They made bows and arrows for shooting birds, and nets and baskets for catching fish and shellfish. They made dugout canoes for paddling.

They had domesticated (tamed) dogs, which enabled them to hunt animals such as deer, elk, and wild boar. These people had better tools than their predecessors. They used spear throwers, devices that fired spears farther.

Music was an important part of people's lives. They kept time in ritual dances with drums and flutes. At Star Carr in Yorkshire, archaeologists have discovered more than 20 masks or headdresses made from deer skulls. Shamans probably wore these during rituals to enter a trance and come closer to the animals or the spirit world.

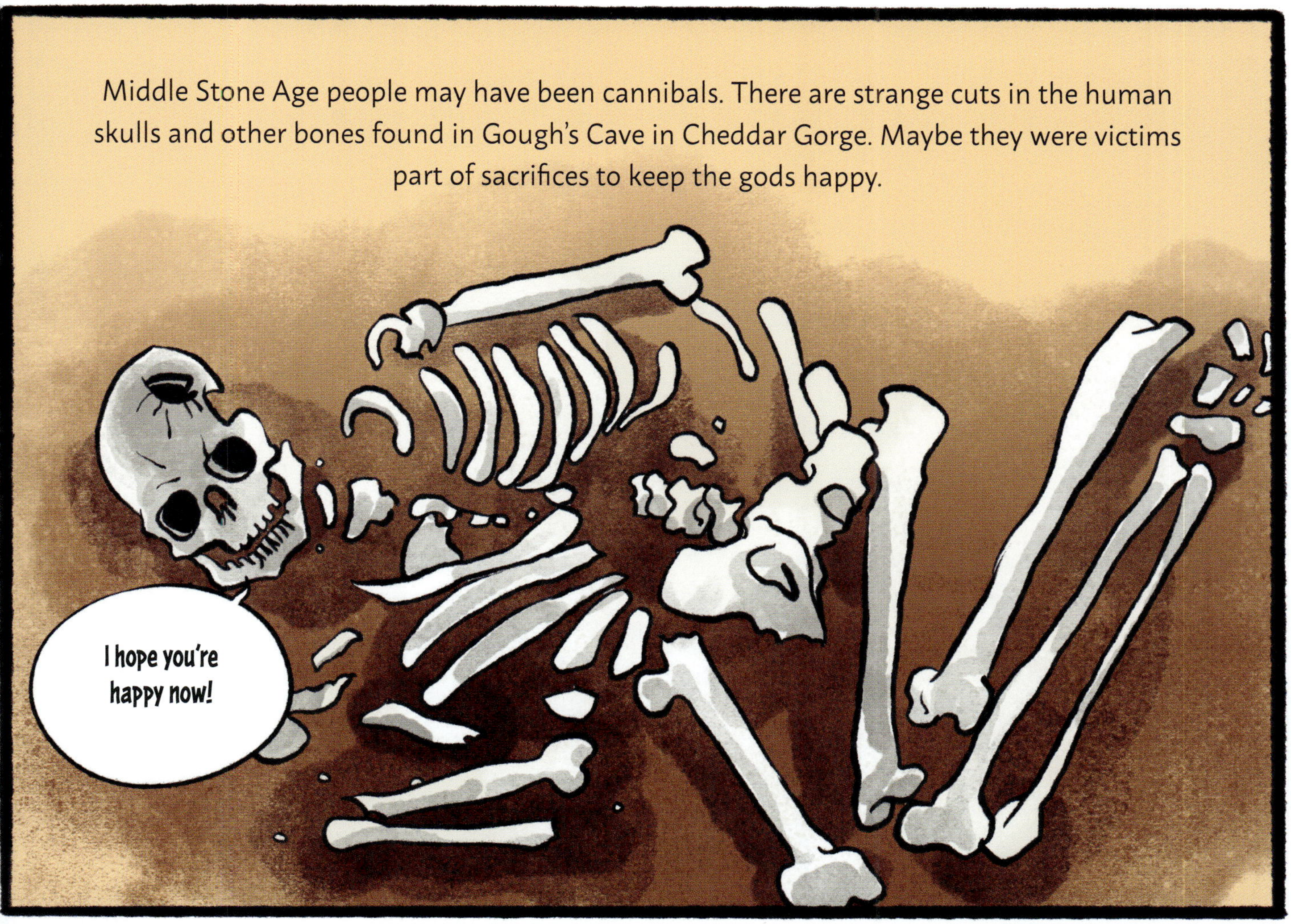

Middle Stone Age people may have been cannibals. There are strange cuts in the human skulls and other bones found in Gough's Cave in Cheddar Gorge. Maybe they were victims part of sacrifices to keep the gods happy.

I hope you're happy now!

Another theory is that their brains had been eaten by the living, thinking it would allow their ancestors' spirits to live on. Some skulls were shaped into cups, which were probably used to hold blood, wine, or food.

If you don't eat your brains, you're not getting any dessert!

WHAT DID PEOPLE DO IN THE NEW STONE AGE?

People in Britain took up farming in the New Stone Age (around 4000 to 2400 BCE). They cleared trees with polished stone axes and planted crops, bringing seeds from mainland Europe.

People learned how to sow, harvest, and store crops.

They also brought over sheep and cows, and tamed native wild boar into pigs.

One of the best-preserved New Stone Age villages is Skara Brae on Orkney Mainland in today's Scotland, which was inhabited from about 3200 to 2500 BCE. Its eight houses were built sunk into the ground to protect against the cold. Their roofs had whalebone or timber frames and were covered with moss or turf.

People spent a lot of time farming and preparing food. Grinding grain to make flour for bread was backbreaking work.

People still made hand axes and other tools from stone and bone, but they became choosier about their materials.

In places where there was good-quality flint, people dug mines. These mines were dangerous places.

Sometimes one shaft was kept as a shrine, where people could make offerings to the gods. They might have asked to be kept safe or for luck finding good stones. Miners traded their flint for other goods.

WHAT WERE STONE AGE TOMBS LIKE?

In their settled villages, New Stone Age people began to take more care over how they buried their dead. They dug underground tombs and marked burial sites with dolmens, mounds, or barrows.

Dolmens consisted of a few huge stone slabs that supported a flat stone, known as the capstone. People erected dolmens all over Europe and the British Isles.

Not all dolmens have human remains under them. The ones that were not tombs might have been put up as markers to show that a particular family lived on and farmed that area of land.

One of the grandest mounds is the one at Newgrange in County Meath, Ireland. Built about 3200 BCE, it measures 250 feet (76 m) across and has a wall running round the edge. A passage leads to a central chamber, which has smaller chambers leading off it.

Newgrange was probably used for special ceremonies. It was designed so that at dawn on the winter solstice, a beam of sunlight shone through an opening above the entrance and lit up the main chamber. New Stone Age people must have understood how the position of the sun in relation to the Earth changed over a year.

Barrows were simple mounds, covering just one burial chamber. Long barrows, named for their oval or rectangular shape, might cover a group of tombs.

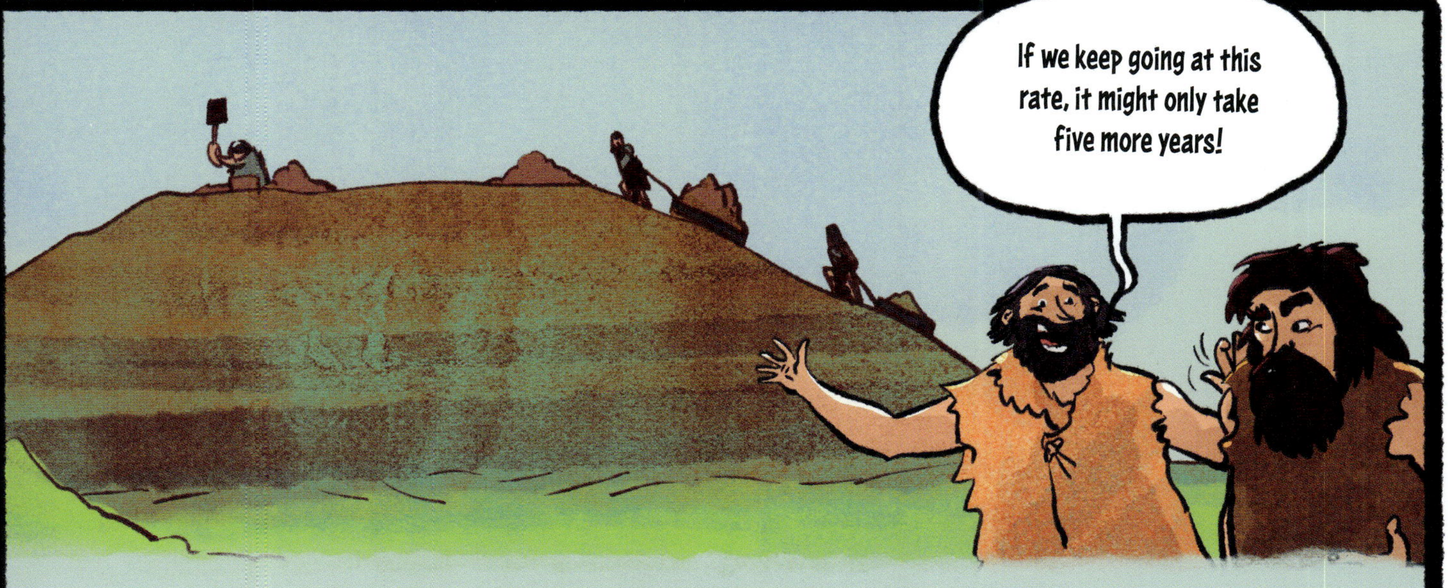

If we keep going at this rate, it might only take five more years!

Silbury Hill is the tallest human-made mound in Europe at 131 feet (40 m) high. It would have taken a team of 500 workers about 10 years to build.

Why was Stonehenge built?

Stonehenge is Britain's most famous prehistoric site. However, exactly why the circle of standing stones was erected and how it was used remains a mystery.

Over the years, people have suggested that the monument might have been a temple, a burial site, a healing center, or even a kind of calendar.

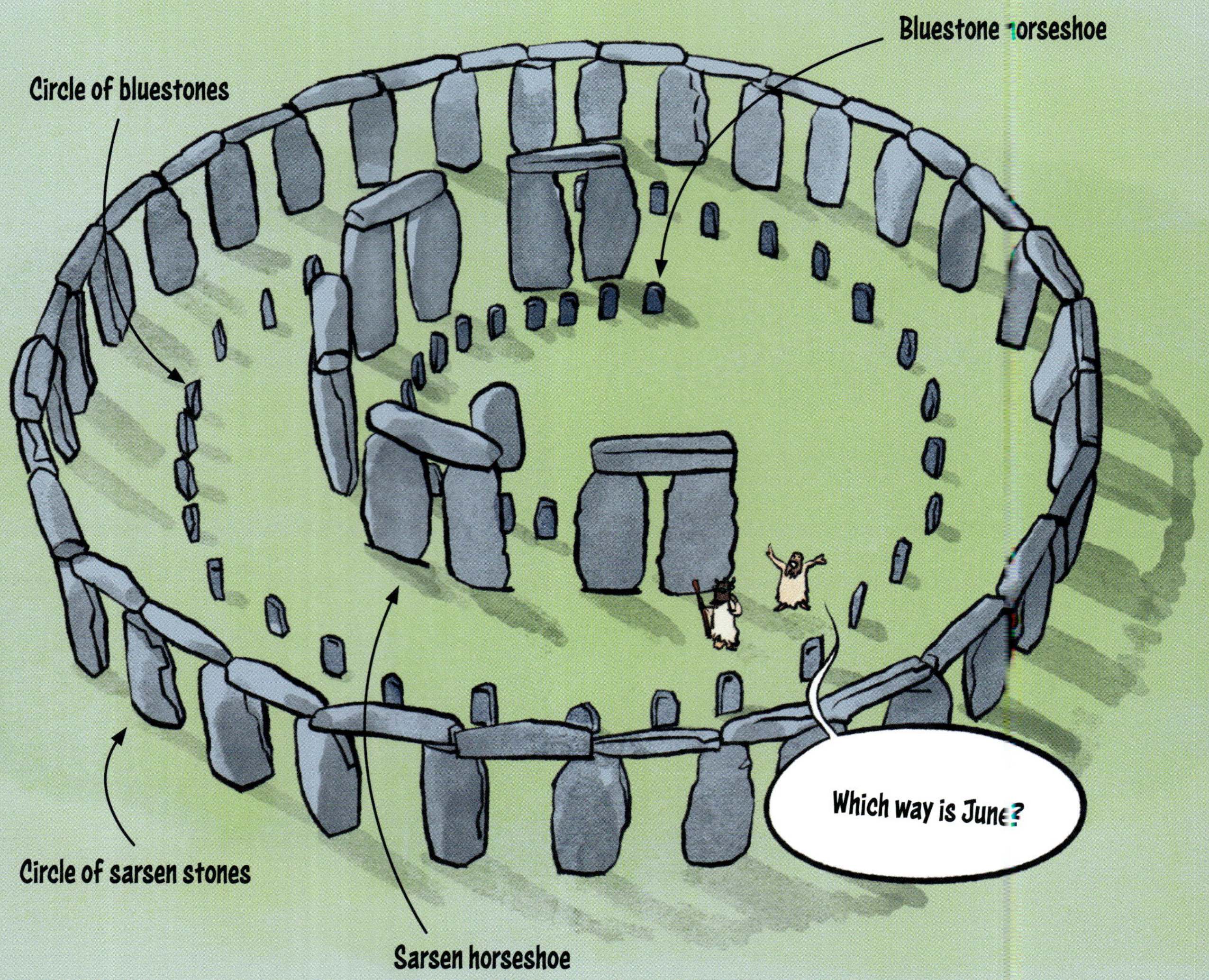

Stonehenge was built in stages over about a thousand years. The first stage began around 3000 BCE, when people dug a circular ditch and bank. This kind of earthwork is called a henge. Small pits inside the henge were dug to bury people's ashes after they had been cremated. Some of these pits contain grave goods.

There are two types of stone at Stonehenge. The smaller ones, known as bluestones, went up around 2600 BCE. They came from the Preseli Hills in southwest Wales more than 156 miles (250 km) away.
Cheer up! Only a few more miles to go!

They were probably transported using rafts along rivers and rollers on land. The larger stones, known as sarsen stones, were dragged from the Marlborough Downs using sledges and ropes. Each weighed about 27.5 tons (25 mt).

The stones at Stonehenge were carefully positioned. At dawn on the summer solstice, the sun rose to the northeast of the circle. At midwinter, the sun set in the southwest, between the gap in the central horseshoe.

When Did the Bronze Age Begin?

The Bronze Age was the period of history when people began to make things out of metal. In Britain, it started around 2500 BCE. But the first metal that people learned to work was actually copper, not bronze.

After people had learned to shape copper, they began to use tin and gold. By about 2150 BCE, they discovered that copper and tin could be mixed to make a stronger metal: bronze. To feed the demand for bronze, more mines opened up.

Copper load of that!

There were large copper mines at Great Orme in North Wales and in Ireland at Ross Island, County Kerry, and Mount Gabriel, County Cork. There were tin mines in Cornwall and Devon.

Metals were used for useful objects, such as tools and containers, and also for display objects. People could show off their high status by wearing fine brooches and bracelets. The most ornate pieces were made of sheet metal that was hammered into shape as it was cooling. The spectacular golden cape discovered at Mold in Wales was made of sheet gold.

Sure, it looks good, but is it comfy?

WHO WERE THE BEAKER PEOPLE?

The Beaker people appeared in western Europe around 2800 BCE. They made tools, weapons and jewelry, also often found in their burials. They traded the objects they made and their culture spread.

The Beaker people are named after the bell-shaped beakers they also made, which were decorated with lines. Their beakers were used to hold mead (a honey drink) and beer, food, metal ore, and even human ashes.

A man known as the Amesbury Archer was buried with five Beaker pots near Stonehenge around 2300 BCE. There were also clothes, tools, and weapons. By examining his DNA, scientists discovered that the Amesbury Archer had grown up in the Swiss Alps.

Beaker culture only flourished in Britain until about 1700 BCE, but trade links with Europe continued. A wooden boat discovered near Dover dates to the 1500s BCE. Made of oak planks, it would have been used to ferry tin, bronze, and other goods across the English Channel.

It better be, or I'm ditching these guys.

This is going to be our last ditch attempt.

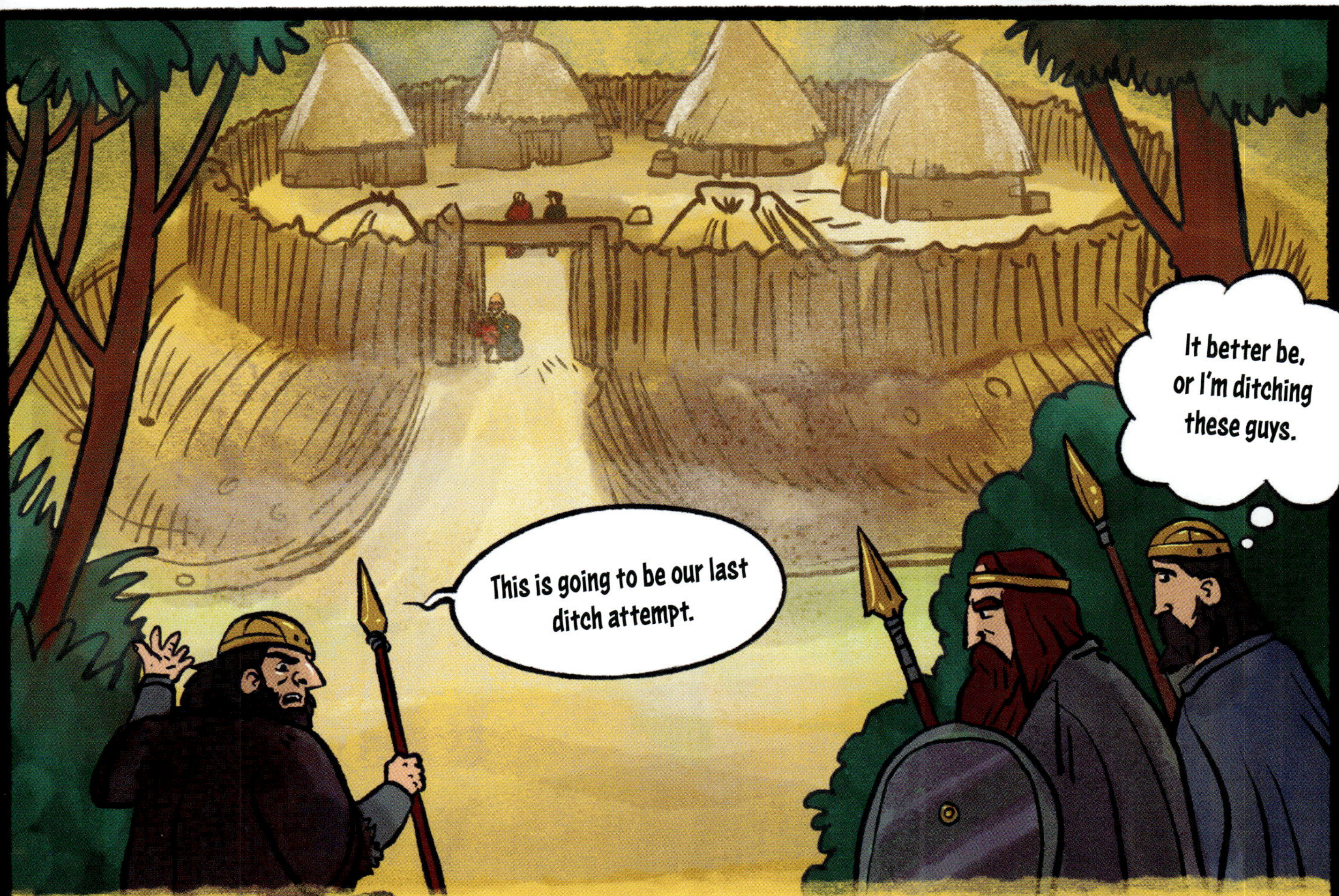

As the Bronze Age continued, there was increasing violence in Britain. Chiefs grew rich and powerful through trade or mining, and fights over territory and resources became common. To protect themselves from raids, people built defensive ditches around their villages.

WHEN DID PEOPLE LEARN TO MAKE IRON?

The first iron objects were made in Britain about 1000 BCE, and by 800 BCE iron had become the main metal being worked. This date marks the start of the Iron Age.

Iron ore was more common than copper or tin so it was easier to find, but the metal itself was harder to extract. It needed hotter temperatures and, often, repeated heating and hammering.

Things might have to get a little heated in here

Within a few hundred years, most tools in Britain were made of iron, and this led to an amazing increase in food production. Using iron axes, farmers could clear greater numbers of trees; with iron shovels and plows they could cultivate heavier soils.

Like a knife through butter!

What's a knife?

They were sowing improved varieties of barley and wheat that yielded bigger harvests. Farmers also planted more peas, beans, flax, and other crops.

Iron Age people did not just change the landscape through farming. They also built nearly 3,000 hill forts across Britain. These were hilltop settlements, protected by ditches and banks.

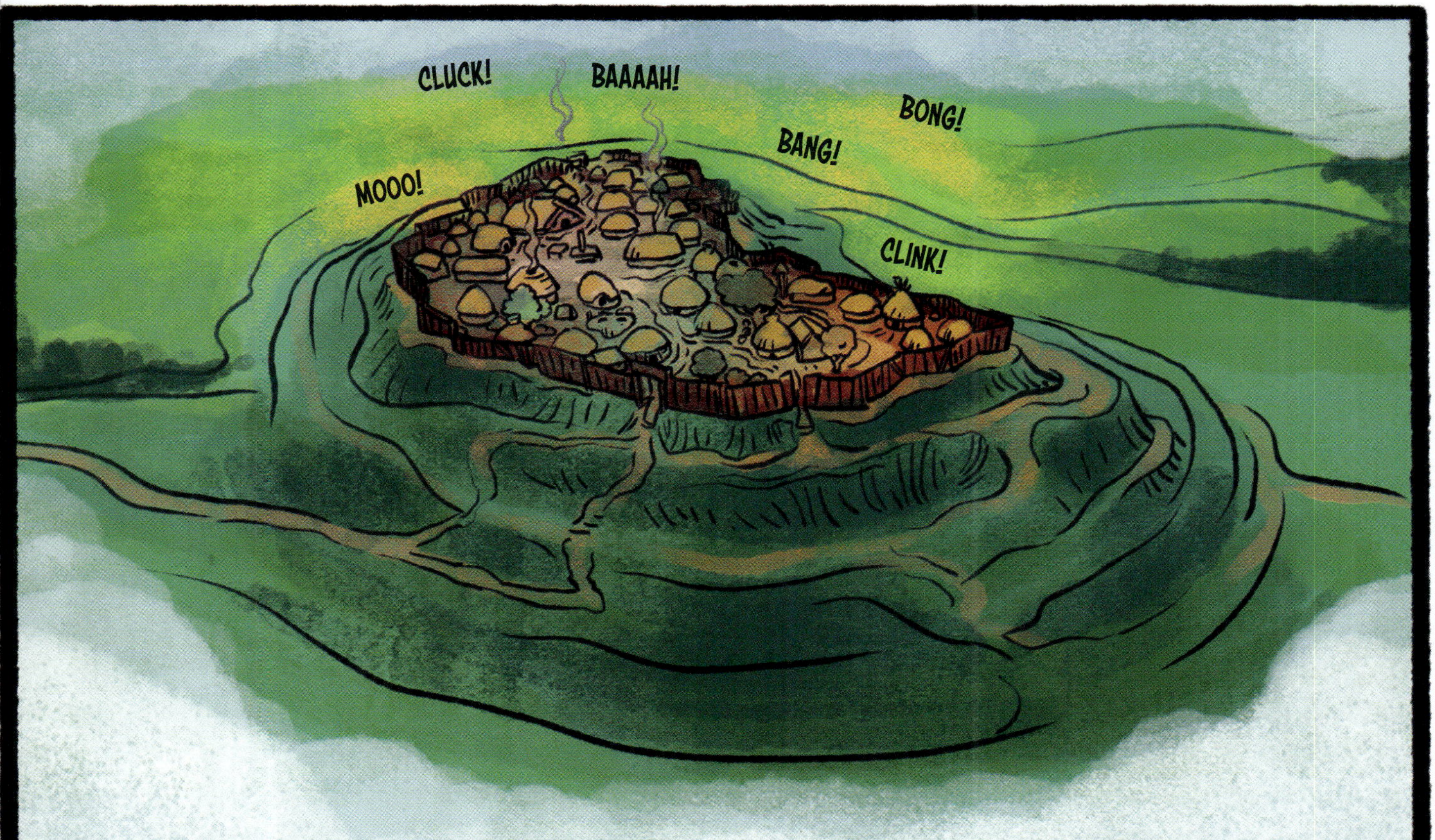

CLUCK! BAAAAH! BONG! BANG! MOOO! CLINK!

Some hill forts were only used as a safe refuge in time of war but others like Maiden Castle in Dorset were fortified towns where people lived all the time. They were packed with roundhouses, barns for livestock, granaries, forges, and textile workshops. The marketplace sold local produce, as well as pottery, wine, oil, and glassware imported from Europe.

WHAT WERE IRON AGE HOMES LIKE?

Most Iron Age homes were roundhouses. Some had timber frames and wattle-and-daub walls. Others were built from stone. Roofs were thatched or covered with turf.

Inside the home, there was just one circular room. At the center was the hearth fire. There was no chimney, but a lot of the smoke escaped naturally through the thatch. The fire heated and lit the home and was used for cooking too.

Some households had metal cauldrons that could be hung over the fire from a three-legged metal stand. Alongside the fire there was often a small clay oven for baking bread.

When women weren't cooking, grinding grain into flour or helping with the garden or livestock, they wove wool to make warm clothes for all the family. At night the family slept on hay mattresses under wool blankets and animal skins.

In Scotland, people built brochs, or circular stone towers, up to four stories high. These may have been lookout posts, surrounded by smaller roundhouses.

Morning!

Hello!

Hey there!

Hiya!

Scottish wheelhouses were stone buildings with spoke-like walls that divided the space into rooms. The largest were about 37.5 feet (11.5 m) across and housed several families.

WHO WERE THE CELTS?

"Celts" is the name given to lots of scattered tribes that existed across Europe during the Iron Age, including the "Britons" who settled in Britain in about 600 BCE.

The Britons were made up of about 30 different tribes, including the Iceni of eastern England. They all spoke similar languages and shared similar customs. They wore fearsome "war paint"of blue dye extracted from a plant called woad.

Come on! Let's go get 'em!

One sec, I just want to get this contouring right.

The Celts lived in tribal communities where everyone had family ties, and answered to a warrior chief or king. They were successful farmers and their craftworkers produced beautiful metalwork, pottery, and jewelry.

Archaeologists have unearthed many hoards of Celtic treasure: gold and silver coins, torcs (neck rings), bracelets, shields, daggers, and swords. Some were buried in times of danger for protection and others were offerings to the gods.

Celtic burials can often be hard for archaeologists to find, but hundreds have been discovered in Yorkshire, England. The most spectacular are the 20 or so chariot burials, where individuals were buried with their chariots, including a woman.

Bodies preserved in peat bogs tell us a lot about Iron Age people. Clonycavan Man from Ireland and Lindow Man from Cheshire, England, were both in their 20s, victims of ritual murders, and wealthy. Exactly why they were killed is a mystery, but it may have been to please the gods.

WHAT DID THE CELTS BELIEVE IN?

Just as there was no single people called the Celts, there was no single set of Celtic beliefs. However, certain practices and gods were common among many or all tribes.

The Celts worshipped hundreds of gods. Some looked after an aspect of the world such as light, dawn, or thunder. Some were in charge of a particular area of human existence, for example motherhood, warfare, or the afterlife. Several gods were associated with more than one idea.

As farmers, the Celts made offerings to certain gods in the hope that they would bring times of plenty. Sucellus was a god of farming, thunder, and forests, who woke up the earth each spring by striking it with his hammer. Cernunnos, an ancient god who had stag's antlers, was another provider, frequently shown feeding animals.

The Celts also believed in countless minor gods, who inhabited particular rocks, trees, rivers, lakes, or mountains. People gave gifts to these gods, throwing bronze or gold armor into rivers and burying precious jewelry in the earth. They also tossed offerings into waterfalls, wells, and springs, because they thought these places were doors from this world into the next.

The Celts believed that everyone who died went to an afterlife. Oak groves (small woods) were sacred to the Celts, and they performed special rituals there.

They also worshipped in small household shrines as well as larger temples. Roman authors say that priests called druids carried out rituals to help guarantee the people's safety and prosperity.

HOW DID THE IRON AGE END?

In Britain, the Iron Age ended when the Romans arrived, bringing their customs with them and changing the British landscape with their roads, towns, forts, villas, and farms. Celtic culture slowly merged with Roman ideas and practices.

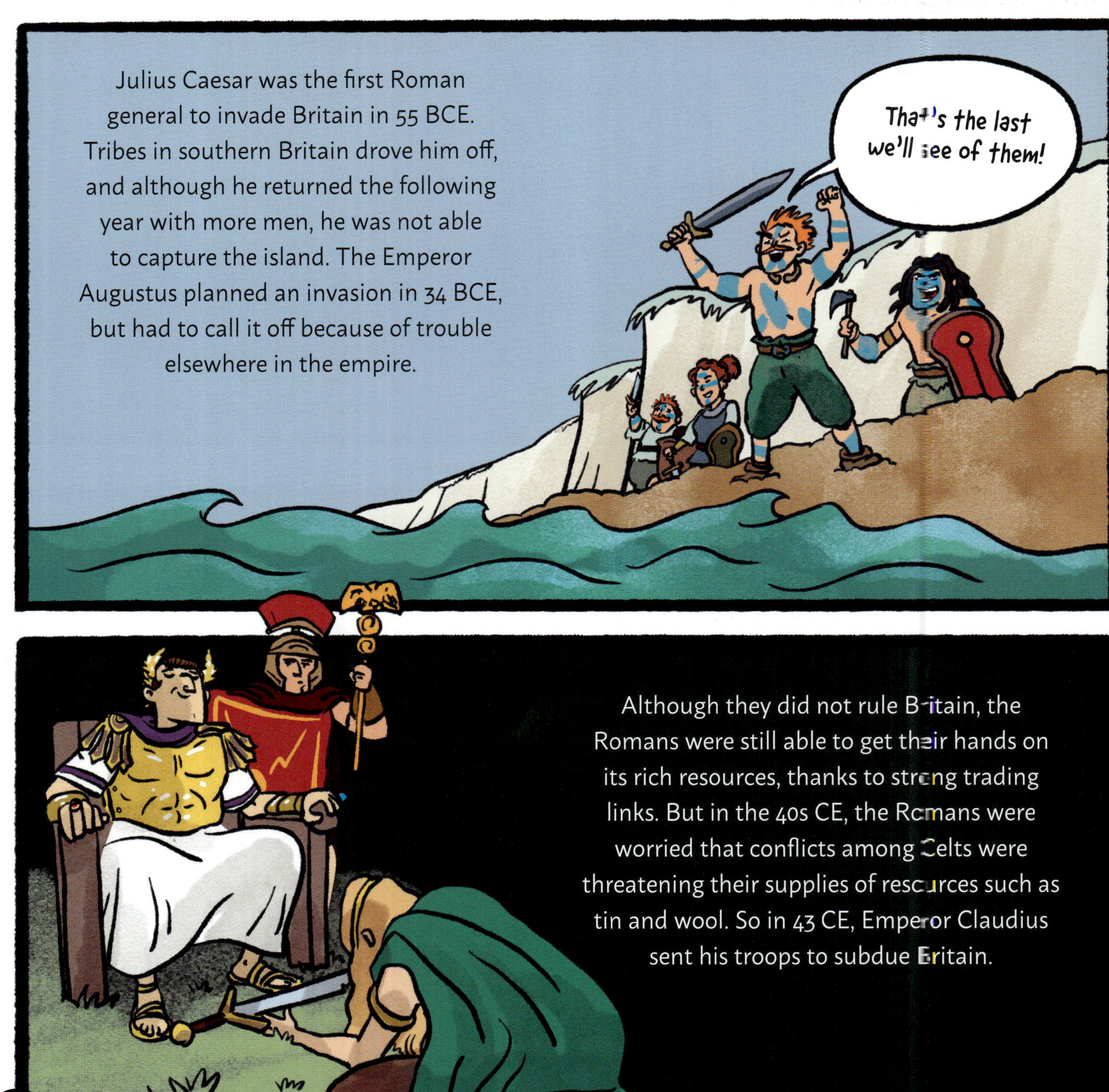

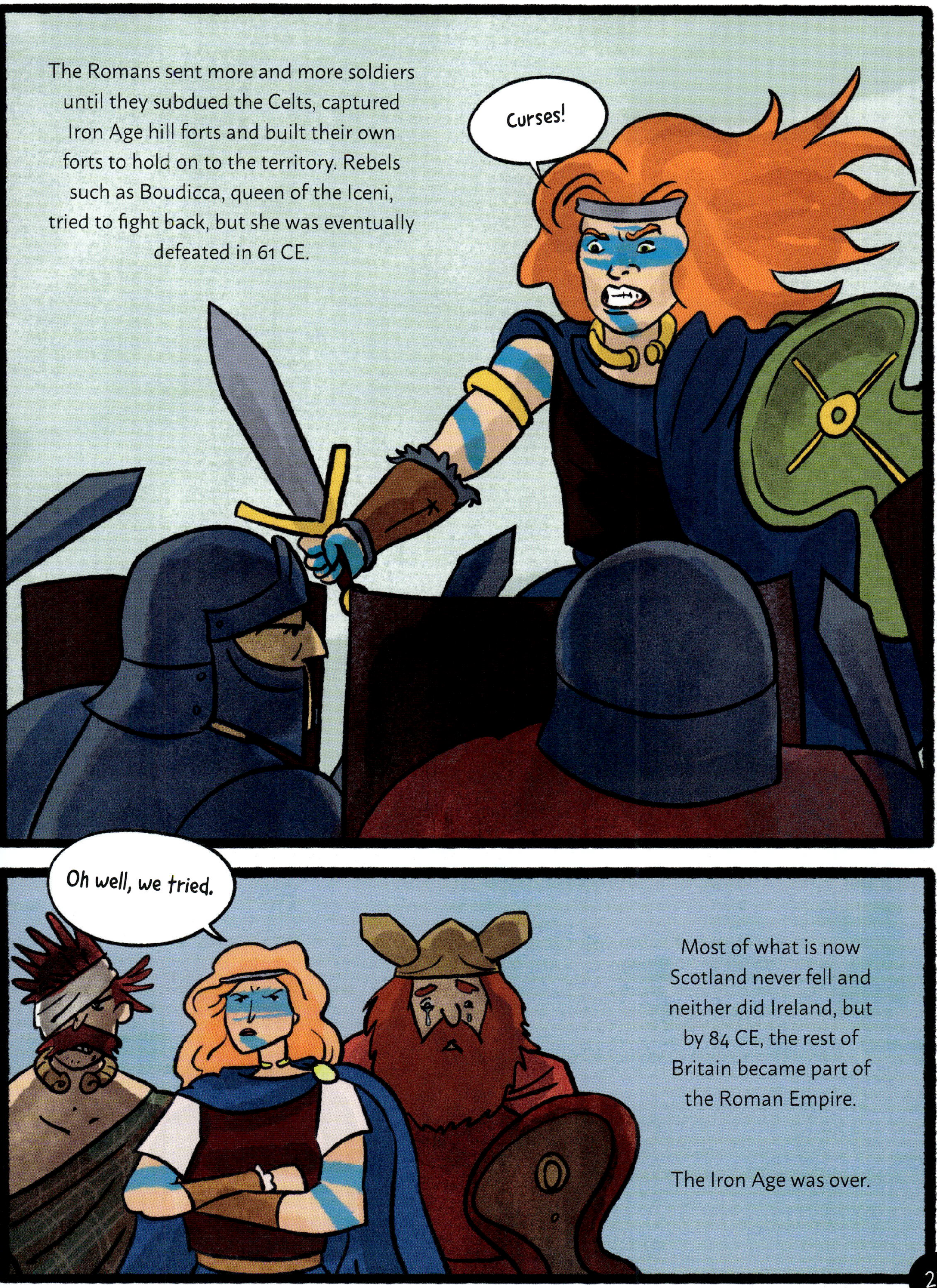

The Romans sent more and more soldiers until they subdued the Celts, captured Iron Age hill forts and built their own forts to hold on to the territory. Rebels such as Boudicca, queen of the Iceni, tried to fight back, but she was eventually defeated in 61 CE.

Curses!

WHAT TO DO NEXT

Now you've learned all these facts about the Stone Age, Bronze Age, and Iron Age, why not try and discover even more?

1

Make your own "Ice Age" engravings by scratching animal outlines onto old pieces of bone or wood. Find out what wild animals lived in your country during the Stone Age.

2

Recreate a prehistoric cave painting using the information you've gathered about the wild animals or reproduce a Celtic pattern on an old T-shirt using clothes dye.

3

Create your own "henge" or dolmen stone monuments using modeling clay or real stones and use lamps to recreate the solstice shining through them.

4

Imagine you are part of Boudicca's Iceni tribe army, preparing to meet the Roman troops. Write a diary of the morning before battle.

5

Draw an aerial plan of an Iron Age hill fort. Label the most important features.

6

For your research, use the internet and your local or school library. Look and see if your local museum has any prehistoric collections.

GLOSSARY

archaeologist Someone who studies the remains of past societies.

barrow A large mound, often built to mark a burial site.

barter To trade by swapping goods, not using money.

BCE "Before the Common Era." Used to signify years before the birth of Jesus, around 2,000 years ago.

Beaker A culture and people in western Europe during the early Bronze Age.

Bronze Age The period when people learned to work metal. In Britain, it lasted from around 2500 to 800 BCE.

CE "Common Era." Used to signify years since the birth of Jesus.

dolmen A Neolithic monument, where a flat stone rests on some upright stones, often built to mark a grave.

druid A Celtic priest.

evolution The process by which living things change over long periods of time and may give rise to new species.

flint A very hard stone.

grave goods Objects placed in tombs for use in the afterlife.

hand axe A cutting tool made from flint, which fits in the hand.

henge A circular ditch and bank of earth built as a monument, sometimes topped with standing stones or wooden pillars.

hoard Buried treasure.

hunter-gatherer Someone who lives by hunting, fishing, and collecting wild foods.

ice age A period when the climate is so cold that ice sheets cover the ground.

Iron Age The period of history when people learned to work iron. In Britain, it lasted from around 800 BCE until the Romans arrived in 43 CE. In Ireland, it lasted until around 400 CE.

Middle Stone Age The period when people were hunter-gatherers using advanced stone tools. In Britain, it lasted from around 9500 to 4000 BCE.

New Stone Age The period when people began to farm. In Britain, it lasted from around 4000 to 2500 BCE. Also known as the Neolithic Age.

Old Stone Age The period when people used simple tools of stone, wood, and bone. In Britain, it lasted from around 800,000 to 11,500 years ago. Also known as the Paleolithic Age.

prehistory The time before written records. In Britain, prehistory ended with the arrival of the Romans in 43 CE.

shaman A tribesperson believed to be in contact with the spirit world.

solstice Midsummer or midwinter.

wattle-and-daub A material used in building walls, consisting of interwoven sticks and twigs covered with mud or clay.

FIND OUT MORE:

Books to read

The Bronze Age by Emma Kaiser (Core Library, 2025)

The Stone Age by Yvette LaPierre (Core Library, 2025)

Stonehenge by Natalie Deniston (Jump!, Inc., 2025)

Websites

https://celts.mrdonn.org/

www.stonepages.com

www.mustfarm.com

Places to visit:

British Museum, London, UK

Museum and Florentine Institute of Prehistory, Florence, Italy

Note to parents and teachers:

Every effort has been made by the publishers to ensure that these websites are suitable for children. However, because of the nature of the internet, it is impossible to guarantee that the contents of these sites will not be altered. We strongly advise that internet access is supervised by a responsible adult.

INDEX